D0363787

Mr. R. Hawkins
46 Birch Grove
Dunfermline
Fife
KY11 8BE

T.B26/AM16.

BRITISH TROLLEYBUSES IN COLOUR

Kevin McCormack

Ian Allan PUBLISHING

End of the Line
Front cover: Reading 120 belonged to a batch of 25 Park Royal-bodied
AEC 661Ts introduced in 1939 to see off the last trams. This view dating
from 1957 also depicts a much longer vehicle, Sunbeam F7 No 174.
Marcus Eavis

The First shall be Last
Back cover: Bradford and neighbouring Leeds opened Britain's first two
trolleybus systems in 1911; Bradford's was also the last. No 844, a former
Mexborough & Swinton single-decker rebodied by East Lancs in 1962,
had the honour of being Britain's final trolleybus to operate (outside
preservation circles). The date is 24 March 1972. *Marcus Eavis*

Green Scene
Title page: Derby's trolleybus livery blends well with the surroundings in
this 1967 view. The vehicle is No 229, a Willowbrook-bodied Sunbeam F4
built in 1952. *Marcus Eavis*

First published 2004

ISBN 0 7110 3008 1

Published by Ian Allan Publishing

an imprint of Ian Allan Publishing Ltd, Hersham, Surrey KT12 4RG.
Printed by Ian Allan Printing Ltd, Hersham, Surrey KT12 4RG.

Code: 0402/B

Introduction

The electric trolleybus or 'rail-less tram' is a mode of transport largely
forgotten in Britain today, except perhaps to the enthusiasts who mourn its
passing and to those visiting working transport museums such as Sandtoft
and Carlton Colville.

The trolleybus served this country for 61 years, from 1911 to 1972,
during which time there were 50 operators, mainly municipal (local
authority). There was a fair spread of systems across England, particularly
in the Midlands and North, and five systems in Wales, but only two in
Scotland and one in Ireland. London had the largest fleet, with over 1,800
vehicles, but, although a trolleybus was demonstrated as early as 1909, it
was 1931 before the first trolleybus entered service there, and they never
really penetrated Central London.

Many operators saw the trolleybus as an economical means of replacing
the tram because, in the early days, they were more reliable and durable
than buses and also the electric infrastructure could be re-used. They shared
with buses the advantage of being able to reach the kerb to pick up and set
down passengers, letting other traffic overtake, but, unlike contemporary
motor buses, they were smooth, quiet and pollution-free. So why were they
eradicated, and why have trams returned to the streets? In the end, buses
proved to be operationally more flexible than trolleybuses. Also, once
operators started to abandon their systems, the cost of new vehicles and
spare parts increased. In addition, electricity became less cheap and
maintenance of the overhead wires more expensive. However, the return of
the trams (with the exception of Blackpool, which never abandoned them)
is curious. Maybe it comes down to fashion. The concept of rapid-transit
systems, largely separated from other road traffic, has simply caught on.
Tracks, previously regarded as an obstacle, are now desirable as a means of
creating this division.

Once upon a time — on 4 September 1962, to be precise — I was sitting
on top of a pillar box, watching the farewell tram procession leaving
Dalmarnock depot in Glasgow. I had witnessed the demise of the London
trolleybus system on 8 May 1962 and surmised then that Glasgow would
be the last trolleybus system and that trolleybuses were bound to run there
for many more years. How wrong I was! By 1967 they had gone, leaving
nine other operators to keep the juice flowing for a little longer.

All 38 trolleybus systems which saw the end of World War 2 (in 1945)
are covered in this book, and no vehicle type is shown more than once
other than to illustrate a livery change. Photographic coverage is from 1949
to 1972, and some of the older vehicles portrayed here have probably never
previously been seen in colour. An index of systems illustrated, with
closure dates, appears on page 80.

It would have been impossible to produce this album without the help of the following photographers who have kindly let me use their material (all, I believe, hitherto unpublished): Marcus Eavis, Harry Luff, C. Carter, Bruce Jenkins and Nick Lera. I am particularly grateful to Martin Jenkins for loaning me transparencies from the Online Transport Archive, a repository for donated and bequeathed cine film, colour transparencies and monochrome negatives. Thanks go also to the Light Rail Transit Association (London Area) for the pictures from the Jack Wyse collection and to John May for certain factual information.

This book complements my bus title *The Heyday of the Half-cab*, published by Ian Allan in 2002, which covers a similar period and features some of the same operators.

Kevin R. McCormack
Ashtead, Surrey
August 2003

Spanish Acquisition
Above: New as No 24 in Rotherham's fleet, this 1951 Daimler CTC6, bodied by East Lancs, became No 1, in which guise it served for four years before being sold to San Sebastian in 1960. *Chris Bennett and Martin Jenkins, Online Transport Archive*

Short and Sweet
Right: Compared with Manchester's three-axle giants, this 54-seater Crossley TDD4, built in 1939, is a midget. No 1166 was withdrawn in 1960 and is pictured here in the previous year. *Chris Bennett and Martin Jenkins, Online Transport Archive*

Going Spare
This 1950 scene in Market Street, Darlington, depicts No 11, an East Lancs-bodied Karrier E4S of 1942 vintage which was sold to Bradford in 1954 for spares. No 5, standing behind, had better luck. It went to Bradford in 1957 and was rebodied as a double-decker, running until 1971. *C. Carter*

Love it or Loathe it
Ashton-under-Lyne's vehicles had an unusual colour scheme, although this
1949 view in Fairfield Street, Manchester shows a simplified version.
Standing alongside a superb Rover car, with a wonderful array of posters
as a backdrop, is No 53, a 1940-built Crossley. *C. Carter*

Imminent Reform

Above: The sign above the doorway is particularly apt, for the St Helens system was about to close when this picture was taken in 1958. However, trolleybus No 385, an East Lancs-bodied BUT 9611T dating from 1951, was too young to die and would see further service in Bradford. *Harry Luff*

Job-sharers

Right: Wolverhampton and Walsall operated trolleybuses jointly between the two towns until 1967, when the Wolverhampton system closed. This view depicts Wolverhampton No 645, a Park Royal-bodied Guy BT, pursued by Walsall No 307, a Weymann-bodied Sunbeam W4 acquired from Hastings. *Marcus Eavis*

All-electric

Left: Ipswich was unique in having a 100%-trolleybus fleet following tram abandonment, until the first buses were purchased in 1950. Displaying the unusual combination of green paint and unpainted aluminium peculiar to Ipswich is No 123, one of 12 Park Royal-bodied Sunbeam F4s dating from 1950. *Marcus Eavis*

Small is Beautiful

Above: Maidstone was a small system of barely seven route miles and had no need for 72-seater monsters. Here is an elderly Park Royal utility-bodied Sunbeam W4 from 1943. *Harry Luff*

9

Old Branding

Above: Nearly 30 years after tram operations ceased in 1929, trolleybus No 21 proudly carries the Hastings Tramways fleetname. A subsidiary of Maidstone & District since 1935, Hastings Tramways lost its maroon livery in favour of its owner's green and cream colours. The Park Royal-bodied Sunbeam W shown here started life in 1946 and would see further service in Bradford. *Marcus Eavis*

Matching Morris

Right: Colour co-ordination between trolleybus and car could not be better in this view at Grimsby Old Market Place in 1957, soon after the Grimsby and Cleethorpes transport fleets officially merged. No 160 was one of four BUT 9611Ts with Northern Coachbuilders bodies which entered service with Cleethorpes in 1950. *J. Copland, courtesy Martin Jenkins*

First Incarnation

Above: This Roe utility-bodied Sunbeam W was new in 1945, rebuilt in 1959 and rebodied in 1962, remaining in service until 1969. As its archaic title suggests, the Teesside Railless Traction Board, owned jointly by Middlesbrough Corporation, Stockton Corporation and Eston Urban District Council, operated one of the first trolleybus systems (from 1919), which was also the penultimate to close. *C. Carter*

Bad Turn

Right: No marks for setting the blinds of Doncaster No 335 as it stands at North Bridge in 1950. The vehicle is actually operating the route to Bentley, which in 1956 was the first trolleybus service to be withdrawn. No 335 was a Roe-bodied Karrier E6 dating from 1935 and was withdrawn in early 1954. *C. Carter*

London Lookalike

Above: The design will be familiar to londoners as pure 'Q1', although the livery has more in common with Glasgow which also bought 'Q1s' (see page 74). The 50 Metro-Cammell-bodied BUT 9641s of 1950, of which No 579 was the first, were Newcastle's last trolleybuses to enter service. This picture was taken in Jesmond Road in July 1955. *Bruce Jenkins*

Capital Asset

Right: Cardiff was the last Welsh operator to retain a trolleybus fleet. On the brow of the hill is No 281, a BUT 9641T with 72-seat East Lancs bodywork from the final batch of double-deckers which entered service in 1955. *Marcus Eavis*

Cheap Win

Above: Advertising a good way to spend a penny, South Shields No 244 carries its 17 years well in this 1963 view. A Roe utility-bodied Karrier W4, it lasted through to the abandonment of trolleybuses in the following year. *J. Copland, courtesy Martin Jenkins*

Born Too Late

Right: The last new trolleybuses to be delivered to a British operator were the Weymann-bodied Sunbeam MF2Bs for Bournemouth, some of which had a working life of less than seven years. The final members of the class were delivered in October 1962, but this view records an earlier example, No 272, at Iford in April 1969. *Marcus Eavis*

Dented Pride

Left: A vicious assault on its Crossley bodywork has spoiled the smart appearance of Bradford Karrier No 691, built in 1940 and rebodied in 1952. *Harry Luff*

Safety in Numbers

Above: April 1962 sees two 1939/40-built London trolleybuses, 'K1' Leyland No 1146 and 'L3' AEC/Metro-Cammell No 1472, sneaking past a prowling lion in London Road, Isleworth. The beast is guarding the 1773-built entrance arch to Syon House. *Nick Lera*

Fading Out
No 15, one of Grimsby's 10 Roe-bodied AEC 664Ts from 1936, is in need
of a repaint and will shortly appear in the new purple livery. This rare shot
was taken in 1951 in Victoria Street South. *C. Carter*

Sea Change

New in 1945 and photographed four years later in Southchurch Avenue, Southend-on-Sea, this Park Royal-bodied Sunbeam W migrated northwards to Doncaster in 1953. On arrival it received a new Roe body which would be transferred to a Doncaster motor bus in 1961, when the trolleybus was withdrawn. *C. Carter*

Grown Up

Left: Having spent six years as a single-decker, this 1950-built Daimler received a new Roe double-deck body in an attempt by Rotherham to make trolleybus operations more economic. No 31 was one of 20 such conversions. *Harry Luff*

Back to Front

Above: The Willowbrook bodywork on Walsall's 22 Sunbeam F4As produced between 1954 and 1956 was distinctive, but some observers unkindly commented that the bodies had been fitted the wrong way round! No 857 is seen in June 1970. *Marcus Eavis*

Putting on the Style
Kingston-upon-Hull adopted a progressive livery which would not look out of place today. Illustrating the innovative design is No 70, a long-serving Brush-bodied Sunbeam built in 1945 and withdrawn in 1963. *Harry Luff*

Watch the Birdie
South Lancashire Transport crew pose in front of their elderly vehicle,
Leyland TTB4 No 59 dating from 1939, in this early-1956 scene.
The SLT system operated into Bolton and also into St Helens, where the
overhead was shared. *Jack Batty, copyright Martin Jenkins*

Public-Private Partnership

Left: An early example of this concept is illustrated in this August 1955 view of Brighton Corporation No 6, a Weymann-bodied AEC 661T from 1939, which carries a company fleetname and a Corporation crest. Brighton, Hove & District and Brighton Corporation shared the trolleybus system, with the former providing one-fifth of the fleet and paying for its use of the Corporation's overhead. *Bruce Jenkins*

Centre of Attraction

Above: Holidaymakers flock to the seaside at Cleethorpes, brought by one of Grimsby's 10 AEC 664Ts which were bodied by Roe and fitted with centre entrance and staircase. This picture dates from August 1955, almost 18 months before the Grimsby and Cleethorpes fleets merged. *Bruce Jenkins*

Must Try Harder

Above: No 17 belonged to Teesside's first batch of double-deck trolleybuses introduced in 1944. In 1958 the operator carried out some modest modernisation by fitting rubber-mounted windows, as seen here, but this was clearly not enough, and four years later the Weymann-bodied Sunbeam W received a radical makeover. Turn to page 42 to see the end result. *Harry Luff*

Built like a Battleship

Right: Unlike the wartime utility bodies, the Cravens coachwork on these AEC 661Ts at Portsmouth Dockyard in 1960 was designed for longevity and lasted some 24 years, until the system was abandoned in 1963. Remarkably, these pristine vehicles dated from 1936/7, when they replaced Portsmouth's last trams. *Marcus Eavis*

All Aboard
Walsall No 225 ranks high in the popularity stakes in this 1949 photograph
at Wolverhampton (whose brand-new Guy No 474 stands behind).
A Park Royal-bodied Sunbeam W built in 1943, it looks superb in its
two-tone blue livery. *C. Carter*

Dirty Look
With only a year or so of trolleybus operations remaining, Llanelly looks
to have lost interest in the appearance of this 1946-built Karrier W4,
No 48, seen outside the railway station in 1951. However, Bradford took
an interest in the vehicle, rebodying it and running it on its system
until 1970. *C. Carter*

Single-minded

Above: There was no place for the high and mighty at Mexborough &
Swinton, which had an exclusively single-deck fleet. Sharing wires with a
Rotherham Daimler in July 1955 is No 11, a Brush-bodied Sunbeam F5
dating from 1947. Mexborough & Swinton was the last non-municipal
trolleybus operator. *Bruce Jenkins*

Collision Course

Right: It's 27 February 1956 in Wigan Road, Atherton, and the
photographer looks to be in danger of being run over if the driver of
South Lancashire Transport No 9 doesn't turn quickly! The veteran
trolleybus was one of the few unrebuilt examples from a batch of 10
Roe bodied Guy BTXs acquired for the inaugural service in 1930.
Jack Batty, copyright Martin Jenkins

Double Act

Left: The transport departments of Grimsby and Cleethorpes were merged officially on 1 January 1957. Carrying the fleetname 'GRIMSBY-CLEETHORPES TRANSPORT', flanked by twin crests, and wearing the new livery, No 19, a 1947-built ex-Grimsby Karrier W4 with Roe bodywork, stands outside Cleethorpes bathing pool while the towels make their precarious way to the laundry. *Harry Luff*

Loose End

Above: Leaving Maidstone town centre for the immortally named terminus in April 1967 is one of the 12 Roe-bodied Sunbeam W4s introduced in 1946/7. These were the last new trolleybuses purchased by Maidstone. *Marcus Eavis*

High Expectations

Left: Huddersfield's trolleybuses had to be capable of climbing the surrounding hills with ease, and the fleet was composed of formidable vehicles. A typical example, seen in 1959, was No 634, from the final batch of Sunbeams. *Harry Luff*

Hull's Angels

Above: Although Kingston-upon-Hull boasted some of the most modern-looking trolleybuses, with front entrances and twin sets of automatic doors, the Corporation relied heavily on elderly, unrebuilt vehicles, such as this Roe-bodied Sunbeam, No 84. *J. Copland, courtesy Martin Jenkins*

Where's the Pedal ?

Left: With its driver apparently preoccupied with his feet, Glasgow TB39 is (hopefully) stationary, a victim of indiscriminate parking. Photographed at George Square in September 1966, this trolleybus belonged to a batch of 90 BUT 9613Ts with Crossley bodies which entered service in 1958/9, some being used for tram replacement. *Bruce Jenkins*

The Great Escape

Above: Intended for Johannesburg but likely to have ended up at the bottom of the sea, 'SA3' No 1752 was one of 43 trolleybuses bound for South Africa but diverted to London in 1942, becoming the capital's first 8ft-wide Public Service Vehicles. An AEC with Metro-Cammell bodywork, No 1752 was photographed at Chadwell Heath in 1959, shortly before withdrawal. *Marcus Eavis*

No Parallel Running

Although the prospect of two trolleybuses running abreast is an exciting one, this photograph is an illusion. The blue Ashton vehicle is stationary — and somewhat better-parked than the Manchester Crossley Empire in the foreground. No 1233 dates from 1950 and is seen at Manchester Piccadilly in June 1958. *Bruce Jenkins*

Fare Shares
As in the picture opposite, more joint working is taking place, this time
involving Walsall and Wolverhampton. Walsall No 343, a Brush-bodied
Sunbeam F4 dating from 1950, has so far avoided the new livery of all-over
blue in this view at St James Square, Wolverhampton. *Bruce Jenkins*

Teesside Sunset

Above: With just over six months to go before closure in April 1971, two consecutively numbered Sunbeam W4s, sporting new Roe bodies to replace their original utility ones (see page 28), are seen wearing the turquoise livery of Teesside Municipal Transport. This undertaking, comprising the merged interests of three municipalities, had taken over from the Railless Traction Board in 1968. *Marcus Eavis*

Last Chance

Right: Local children take a front-seat farewell ride on a Reading trolleybus on the last day of service, 3 November 1968. The author interrupted his labours at Didcot Railway Centre to travel the short distance to Tilehurst to pay his final respects and to photograph this Park Royal-bodied Sunbeam F7, No 178, one of 12 such vehicles. *Author*

Aye, Aye

Left: Glasgow obtained special authorisation from the Ministry of Transport to operate 10 Burlingham-bodied BUT RETB1s which, at 34ft 6in, exceeded the maximum permitted length for two-axle vehicles; these 50-seaters on route 108 replaced trams on route 12 in 1958. No TBS20 is depicted here in Shields Road in September 1966, heading for the attractively named Mount Florida. *Bruce Jenkins*

Late Starter

Right: Cardiff did not introduce trolleybuses until 1942 and No 208, an AEC 664T with bodywork by Northern Counties, belonged to the initial batch of ten vehicles. It was to be another six years before Cardiff obtained any further trolleybuses. No 208 ran until 1962, while Cardiff's trolleybus network just managed to enter the 1970s. *Harry Luff*

Taking to the Hills

Like Huddersfield's trolleybuses, the Bradford fleet was not confined to urban operation and was also required to climb hills and roam the countryside, as illustrated in this view from September 1970. The vehicle is

No 714, a much-rebuilt Karrier W originating in 1945 and fitted with a new front-entrance body by East Lancs in 1959. *Marcus Eavis*

Missed

Mother and child escape the silent assassin in this rare colour shot at Ilkeston in 1951. The Nottinghamshire & Derbyshire Traction Co was formerly a Balfour Beatty subsidiary, and the system was closed in 1953 despite the retention of Corporation trolleybuses in both Nottingham and Derby. The vehicle shown is No 332, a Weymann-bodied AEC 661T which, together with the remainder of the Notts & Derby trolleybus fleet, was sold to Bradford. *C. Carter*

Rush Hour
There is plenty of activity, both human and vehicular, in this 1950 view
at St Sepulchre Gate, Doncaster. Taking centre stage is a 1939-built
Karrier E6 with Roe bodywork, No 355 (formerly No 55), which lasted
until 1955. *C. Carter*

Extended Life

Above: Bradford extracted 28 years of service from this AEC 661T dating from 1934. However, this was at the expense of its original English Electric body, which was replaced in 1947 by a new one from Northern Coachbuilders. *Harry Luff*

Greenhouse Effect

Right: It is fortunate that window tax had been abolished by the time this Park Royal-bodied Karrier MS2 hit the streets of Huddersfield in 1947! No 541, now preserved, is seen at Longwood. *Harry Luff*

Waiting Time

Left: A long-forgotten type of road sign features prominently in this portrait of Nottingham No 471. The vehicle was one of 10 Karrier W4s with bodies by Park Royal, introduced in 1946. *Harry Luff*

Supporting Act

Above: Portsmouth was renowned for its fleet of 76 prewar Cravens-bodied AECs, which served to the end. Consequently, it is easy to overlook the batch of 15 stylish Burlingham-bodied BUT 9611Ts which entered service in 1950/1. During the final days of operation, in July 1963, No 314 heads for the Dockyard terminus. *Marcus Eavis*

New Kid on the Block

Above: Looking as though it is entering the set of *Coronation Street*, South Lancashire No 70, one of six Weymann-bodied Karrier MS2s built in 1947/8, was ultra-modern compared with the rest of the fleet. This evocative photograph was taken on 27 February 1956 in Mealhouse Lane, Atherton. *Jack Batty, copyright Martin Jenkins*

Lying Low

Right: Preparing to negotiate the low railway bridge in Bute Street, Cardiff, is East Lancs-bodied BUT 9641T No 243. A mere stripling from 1955, it augmented the existing fleet of single-deckers, consisting of five BUT 9641Ts built in 1949. *Marcus Eavis*

Ever Decreasing Circles

Darlington trolleybuses would not be negotiating this roundabout for very much longer because the system was abandoned in July 1957, shortly after this photograph was taken. However, No 4, a Brush-bodied Karrier W from 1944, went on to serve Bradford, being fitted with a new East Lancs body in 1959 and surviving until 1972. *J. Copland, courtesy Martin Jenkins*

Crestfallen

Actually, it was never there to start with, because this is a Brighton, Hove & District trolleybus, not a Corporation one! Further clues are provided by the registration number and limited amount of advertising. Seen at Brighton racecourse in August 1958, Weymann-bodied BUT 9611T No 391 (previously numbered 6391), was built in 1948 and sold in 1959 to Bournemouth, where it served until 1965. *Bruce Jenkins*

Back to Basics

Right: There were no embellishments on the wartime utility vehicles and most operators rebodied them when more stylish designs and more comfortable interiors became available in the 1950s. Derby, however, bucked the trend, and several utility trolleybuses had long working lives, including No 175, seen here in 1960. This Park Royal-bodied Sunbeam W from 1945 was not withdrawn until 1965, when it went for preservation. *Marcus Eavis*

No More Twiddly Bits

Left: Portsmouth's livery as seen on page 29 looks ornate but was nothing compared with the pre-1949 livery carried by the trolleybus fleet (phased out on the bus fleet from 1938). This unique colour shot depicts No 270 with double parallel lining and with more extensive coverage than the later single lining, as well as ornate square corners. *Jack Wyse collection*

Taking its Turn

Right: In the narrow confines of Christchurch, beneath one of the ruins that Cromwell knocked about a bit (!), Bournemouth No 235, a Weymann-bodied BUT 9461T dating from 1950, approaches the famous turntable during the summer of 1966. This was the only means of pointing the vehicle in the return direction, there being no space for a turning circle or even for a three-point turn under battery power. *Marcus Eavis*

Of Great Renown
The magnificent Triumph car almost steals the show in this view at
Parliament Square, Nottingham, in March 1958. But the trolleybus also
deserves a mention: No 491, a Roe-bodied BUT dating from 1948.
Bruce Jenkins

High Voltage
This scene from 1966 shows Manchester Piccadilly railway station, with main-line electrification above and trolleybus electrification below (but not for much longer). The vehicle is No 1328, one of a batch of 62

Burlingham-bodied BUT 9612Ts delivered in 1955/6.
Chris Bennett and Martin Jenkins, Online Transport Archive

Thwarted Springbok

Above: This vehicle, from a batch of 10 8ft-wide Sunbeam MF2s, had a chassis built for service in Johannesburg, South Africa. The chassis never went there and, instead, were fitted with lowbridge Massey bodies in 1942 and delivered to St Helens, a town which had several low bridges until roads were lowered in 1949. Withdrawn at the end of 1955, No 360 was photographed earlier that year. *J. Copland, courtesy Martin Jenkins*

Super Saver

Right: Doncaster was certainly thrifty when it came to running its transport department. Late in 1954, it bought Mexborough & Swinton single-decker No 4 (along with five others), had a new double-deck Roe body fitted and ran the vehicle as No 396 until 1962. Upon withdrawal, the body was converted to half-cab layout and re-mounted onto one of Doncaster's buses. *Harry Luff*

Additional Relief

Above: Teesside Railless Traction Board No 2 displays the earlier livery of white-painted upper-deck window surrounds in this photograph taken in July 1955. No 2 was one of seven Sunbeam F4s purchased in 1950, all of which had their original East Lancs bodywork replaced by Roe between 1962 and 1965. *Bruce Jenkins*

Down in the Mouth

Right: Ashton-under-Lyne's unusual livery, combined with the window design of the Crossley Empires, makes No 78 look decidedly miserable! Built in 1950, this vehicle from a batch of five is seen at Manchester Piccadilly in 1956. *Bruce Jenkins*

Anonymous Owner

Above: Four trolleybuses were bought by South Lancashire Transport in 1936 for the Bolton–Hilton Lane Ends–Atherton service, with Bolton Corporation contributing to the cost. Ownership was transferred to Bolton in 1944, but the vehicles remained in SLT livery. No 48 was the first of the four — all Roe-bodied Leyland TTB4s — and was withdrawn from service just after this photograph was taken on 17 February 1956. *Jack Batty, copy-right Martin Jenkins*

Merger-mad

Right: Having absorbed another of its subsidiaries — Chatham & District — in 1955, Maidstone & District did the same to Hastings Tramways in 1957, applying its fleetname to the trolleybuses, as shown on No 8. This vehicle was a Weymann-bodied AEC 661T new in 1940. In the background is a 1955 Weymann-bodied AEC Reliance of East Kent. *Harry Luff*

Cover-up
Ipswich's trademark aluminium surfaces are not on display here, for this
1938-built Ransomes, Sims & Jefferies trolleybus has a Massey body with
steel panels. Seen in April 1957, No 84 was withdrawn two years later.
Bruce Jenkins

Small-time Operator

At the opposite end of the spectrum from London Transport (which had over 1,800 trolleybuses) was Pontypridd Urban District Council, which had just eight (for its 3.3 route miles). No 12, seen in 1952, was a Park Royal utility-bodied Karrier W4 from 1945. When the system closed in 1957 this trolleybus became No 238 in the South Shields fleet.
C. Carter

Bradford Brilliance

Left: Against a background of dereliction stands another representative from the Corporation's pristine trolleybus fleet. No 753 was a BUT 9611T with 8ft-wide Weymann bodywork, built in 1950 and lasting 20 years. *Harry Luff*

Slim Model

Above: Nottingham purchased a large number of postwar Brush-bodied BUT 9611Ts, mostly 7ft 6in wide, although there were some eight-footers, identifiable by their white steering wheels. Up against AEC Regent bus No 223 in Parliament Square in September 1965, No 581 is definitely of the narrow variety. *Marcus Eavis*

Heave Ho!

Above: South Shields No 254 resists the conductor's efforts to overturn it (well, that's the impression the camera gives) as it waits at the North Sea resort in 1963. The vehicle was a 1947 Karrier W4 bodied by Northern Coachbuilders. *J. Copland, courtesy Martin Jenkins*

Seven-year Switch

Right: Two of Reading's most modern trolleybuses, Burlingham-bodied Sunbeam F4As from 1961, are depicted here in April 1966. When the system closed in 1968, only five trolleybus operators remained, so there was not much of a second-hand market. Nevertheless, five of the dozen class members, including No 184, managed a further three years' service on Teesside. *Marcus Eavis*

Classic Splendour

Left: Most of London Transport's huge trolleybus fleet shared the same well-proportioned design. It is, therefore, befitting that Class L3 No 1445, a Metro-Cammell-bodied AEC, should be photographed against the magnificent backdrop of 18th-century Garrick Lodge, which faces the River Thames at Hampton. This shot was taken a few weeks before closure of the London trolleybus system in 1962. *Nick Lera*

Beauty and the Beast

Above: The old and new liveries of Maidstone Corporation are captured here at Barming as 1944-built Sunbeam W No 56, rebodied by Roe in 1962, passes a brand-new Leyland Atlantean. *Marcus Eavis*

Track Record

Above: Glasgow was the last place where trams and trolleybuses ran together — a situation which lasted from 1949 to 1962. In this scene from 1957, Metro-Cammell-bodied BUT 9641T No TB18, built in 1949 and bearing a strong resemblance to a London 'Q1', passes over the tram tracks. *Marcus Eavis*

Empire-building

Right: Unlike the frowning Crossley-bodied examples in Ashton-under-Lyne, this Cleethorpes Crossley Empire, one of a pair, has a flattering Roe body. Although the body dated from 1951, Walsall was sufficiently impressed to operate the vehicle in its original form for more than 10 years after the Grimsby-Cleethorpes system closed in 1960. No 63 was photographed in August 1955 at the familiar Cleethorpes terminus. *Bruce Jenkins*

Time for a Cuppa

Above: A bus conductor takes his break in front of Ashton No 83, displaying the later livery. A 1956-built BUT 9612T, it was fitted with a body manufactured by the local firm of S. H. Bond. This scene from July 1966 also includes a Manchester BUT 9612T with distinctive Burlingham bodywork. *Marcus Eavis*

Running Repairs

Right: Belfast No 121 creeps past AEC tower wagon No 54 while the overhead receives attention in August 1964. The trolleybus is a Guy BTX dating from 1948 and, like virtually the entire fleet, carried a body built locally by Harkness. *Marcus Eavis*

Early Casualty
Colour photographs of Birmingham trolleybuses are very rare because the system closed in 1951. Pulling out of Carr's Lane in 1949 is No 18, one of 50 Leyland TTBD2s with Metro-Cammell bodywork, dating from 1934. *C. Carter*

Boom and Gloom
De-wired and in the pouring rain stands West Hartlepool No 32, one of 14 Daimler CTM4s bodied by Roe. These vehicles were owned jointly by West Hartlepool County Borough Council and Hartlepool Borough Council, between which towns they plied until closure of the system in 1953.
C. Carter

Heading for Trouble
Displaying Wolverhampton's strangest destination on its blind, No 421
stands at Willenhall in 1950. One of 15 Park Royal-bodied Sunbeam Ws
constructed in 1946, it received a new Roe body in 1958. *C. Carter*

Index of Systems Illustrated, in Order of Closure

Ian Allan
PUBLISHING

Full details of Ian Allan Publishing
titles can be found on
www.ianallanpublishing.com
or by writing for a free copy of
our latest catalogue to:
Marketing Dept, Ian Allan Publishing,
Riverdene Business Park,
Molesey Road, Hersham KT12 4RG.

For an unrivalled range of aviation, military,
transport and maritime publications, visit our secure
on-line bookshop at
www.ianallansuperstore.com

or visit the Ian Allan Bookshops in

Birmingham
47 Stephenson Street, B2 4DH;
Tel: 0121 643 2496;
e-mail: ia-birmingham@btconnect.com

Cardiff
31 Royal Arcade, CF10 1AE;
Tel: 02920 390615;

e-mail: ianallancar@btconnect.com

London
45/46 Lower Marsh, Waterloo, SE1 7RG;
Tel: 020 7401 2100;
e-mail: ia-waterloo@btconnect.com

Manchester
5 Piccadilly Station Approach, M1 2GH;
Tel: 0161 237 9840;
e-mail: ia-manchester@btconnect.com

and (aviation and military titles only) at the **Aviation
Experience, Birmingham International Airport**
3rd Floor, Main Terminal, B26 3QJ;
Tel: 0121 781 0921
e-mail: ia-bia@btconnect.com

or through mail order by writing to:
Ian Allan Mail Order Dept,
4 Watling Drive, Hinckley LE10 3EY.
Tel: 01455 254450.
Fax: 01455 233737.
e-mail: midlandbooks@compuserve.com

You are only a visit away from over 1,000 publishers
worldwide.